SERMON OUTLINES
FOR
Christian Living

GENE WILLIAMS

Beacon Hill Press of Kansas City
Kansas City, Missouri

Contents

PART I
GETTING TO KNOW GOD

Introduction

This series of messages will be looking at different truths about God that will enable the listener to have a better understanding of who He is and what He is like. The more we understand God, the stronger our faith becomes. Strong faith enables us to place complete trust in Him. And complete trust elevates the peace and joy of our lives to a higher level than we ever dreamed. This level of living enables us to lift up Jesus in our daily lives.

These messages do not reflect deep theology. They are, however, theologically correct. They present in a simple, biblical manner concepts about God that will help those who are unable to attend schools of higher learning to grasp some very important truths.

GETTING TO KNOW GOD

Isaiah 6:1-5

Introduction

A. This sermon series will help us have a greater understanding of God. We know that He is, and we accept that truth. We believe that the Bible is His Word. We need to have a greater understanding of Him and His nature.

B. Today, we are looking at a man who, by getting to know God, became "a voice of good news to a world that desperately needed it."
   1. We are looking at the fact that we can know God.
   2. Isaiah was a native of Jerusalem. But it was only after Isaiah came to know God in a personal way that he could reach the pinnacle of his life. He prophesied the birth of Jesus (7:14). He promised guidance in adversity (30:19-21). He announced the Good News in chapters 35, 43, and 53. Read the scripture: Isa. 6:1-5.

C. The longer we live with God, the better we know Him. Still there is a time when our eyes are opened, and we see God as never before. When that happens God becomes more than a word to us. The better you get to know God, the more you love Him.

I. Getting to Know God

A. Some logical questions are: Who is God? What is He like? What does He expect of me?

B. In speaking to Moses, God identifies himself as "I AM" (Exod. 3:14). "I AM" indicates His unsearchableness rather than His existence. God never argues for His existence. The world declares that (Ps. 19).

II. God Gives Insights to His Nature Through His Names

A. Some of God's favorite names include:
   1. Elohim—The power of God used in behalf of people.
   2. Jehovah—The eternal, ever-loving One.
   3. El Shaddai—Almighty, all-sufficient God.

B. Other names are used to define who God is. Unfortunately, God is not a sacred word to a majority of our world. One of the reasons for the degeneration of our society is its failure to recognize and reverence the name of God.

III. We Need to Reemphasize Respect for God
A. We can learn about this from our devout Jewish friends.
1. Some only refer to God as "the Name," feeling unworthy to say "God."
2. In Matt. 5:33-37 Jesus is cautioning us to be careful how we use God's name.
3. Jesus is saying that we must let our characters be such that we do not need to emphasize our truthfulness and honesty by using God's name. Respect God.
B. Read the scripture: Isa. 6:1-8.

IV. In This Passage of Scripture Isaiah Tells of a Special Encounter He Had with God
A. Some scholars think Isaiah may have been a cousin of King Uzziah.
1. His name means "Jehovah is our helper" and "Salvation is of the Lord."
2. What is important in this account is Isaiah's encounter with God.
3. Isaiah had a moment with God that enabled him to make a powerful impact on his world. He saw God in His holiness and realized his unworthiness.
4. His recognition of his need for God's cleansing power moved God to change him.
B. One of the main truths about God that we need to learn is that He is for us. God is violently opposed to sin, and Scripture abounds with illustrations of this. Those who honor His name respect His sovereignty, obey His commands, and see His holiness will discover God to be a Friend. God will give us a reason to live, as He did with Isaiah.

Conclusion
God is not just a word. He is a Father to love and a Friend to experience.

GOD IS A GOOD SHEPHERD

Ezekiel 34:11-25

Introduction
A. It is a wonderful thing when God intervenes in the lives of His people.
B. In our scripture for today humanity has failed to meet the needs of God's people.
   1. God is saying, "I will take that responsibility and come to their aid."
   2. It is important to understand that we serve and worship God—not men.
   3. Today, we are looking at this compassionate, caring God.
   4. Read the scripture: Ezek. 34:11-25.

I. Note the Compassion of God (vv. 11-12)
A. God says, "I will search for my sheep. I will look for them."
B. Jesus describes a shepherd who seeks for one lost sheep (Luke 15). In Ezek. 34:12, God is seeking for His people who have been scattered by a storm.
C. It is important to understand that we do not serve a hard taskmaster but a God of love and compassion.
D. He can deliver His sheep from their difficulties.
   1. "I will rescue them from the places where they were scattered on a day of clouds and darkness" (Ezek. 34:12).
   2. Just as the sheep are safer with a good shepherd and do not run from him, so are we safe in the care of a loving God, and we must not run from Him.

II. Note the Care of God (vv. 14-16)
A. God describes the care of a loving shepherd for his sheep.
   1. He provides a good fold that is safe from ravenous beasts (see John 10:9).
   2. Sheep need good pasture, and He promises to provide this in verse 14.

3. When sheep are hurt, they need to be bound up, not destroyed (v. 16).
4. According to Ps. 23, the shepherd will supply every need of the sheep.
B. God promises to give us exactly what we need.
1. There is wonderful safety in resting in the care of our Good Shepherd.
2. We find an abundance of all that we need for daily living in Him (John 10:10).
3. When needs arise, our Good Shepherd is present to help us face them (Luke 8:40-56).

III. Note the Covenant of God (vv. 22, 25-31)

A. Those who are a part of God's flock not only have His compassion and care but also have a covenant that is a promise from God.
B. God says, "I will save my flock" (v. 22).
1. His flock will no longer be prey for wild beasts (see 1 Pet. 5:8).
2. Before any beast could destroy a good shepherd's flock, it had to destroy the shepherd.
3. Jesus met Satan head on at Calvary and won the battle for us.
C. There will be showers of blessing on the lives of the faithful (v. 26).
1. Our lives will not be like a desert but like a garden.
2. Lives blessed by God are as clean as the air after a spring shower.

Conclusion

A. "They will live in safety, and no one will make them afraid" (Ezek. 34:28b).
1. The sheep were safe, and they were unconcerned because they confidently trusted the shepherd.
2. We may live in that same confidence (Rom. 8:31).
B. David described the confidence that belongs to us in another way (Ps. 23:6).
C. The peace of mind, confidence of soul, and joy for living that all of us want belong to those who are part of the Good Shepherd's flock.

HE IS A GOD WHO HAS GREAT PLANS

Jeremiah 29:11

Introduction

   A. To truly know God, we must remember that He is a God who has great plans.

      1. He planned the universe flawlessly.

      2. He planned the redemption of humankind to perfection.

      3. He has great and wonderful plans for each one of us.

      4. Read the scripture: Jer. 29:11.

   B. When we accept and understand this characteristic of God, our faith in Him and our trust in His guidance are strengthened.

      1. It is easy to trust and believe in someone who has the record of accomplishment that God has.

      2. One of the things we hope to accomplish in this series is to strengthen our faith by looking at Him.

      3. The primary purpose of every Christian is to bring glory to God.

   C. David speaks to this in Ps. 40:1-8.

      1. When we live in verse 8, God is glorified.

      2. There are three things that will help us live in this verse.

I. It Helps Our Faith in God's Plans to Look at His Universe

   A. All of creation interacts in an orderly fashion.

      1. There is no randomness in God's creation. Where things are random, destruction always follows.

      2. Illustration: The planets are lined up in specific order. If one of them should leave its orbit, it would be destroyed.

   B. Read Ps. 19:1-11.

      1. God does not try to prove His existence.

      2. He lets the meticulously planned universe speak for Him.

   C. Another simple truth speaks of God's plan—the food chain.

      1. Illustration: Insects feed fish and then fish become food for us.

      2. This sequence of events did not happen by chance.

II. It Helps Our Faith to Consider His Plan for Our Redemption

    A. Adam and Eve chose to stray from God's plan.

        1. Every pain and problem we experience are results of that decision.

        2. Planets and meteorites that break loose from God's plan are destroyed.

        3. God has better plans for us than pain and weeds.

    B. God's love for His highest order of creation compelled Him to act.

        1. "The Lamb that was slain from the creation of the world" (Rev. 13:8).

        2. In the very beginning, God knew His plans for a perfect world would have problems when He gave humankind freedom. So at creation He provided an option for those who would choose a better plan.

        3. Jesus came "when the time had fully come" (Gal. 4:4).

III. It Helps Our Faith to Remember That He Has Great Plans for Each One of Us Individually

    A. Read the scripture again (Jer. 29:11).

        1. God has better plans for most of us than we could ever design for ourselves.

        2. Illustration: Dwight L. Moody had plans to be a shoe salesman in Chicago. God made him into one of the greatest evangelists of all times.

        3. Give your personal testimony of how God led you into the ministry.

    B. Some of God's plans are beyond our comprehension, but they always work.

        1. Illustration: According to scientific knowledge, bumblebees cannot fly. But they do fly because of God's plan.

        2. Everything in God's highly organized world functions according to His design work. So will His plans for you and me.

Conclusion

    A. God has great plans for you. So, take courage and hope.

    B. Make the most of your life and opportunities to bring glory to the Creator of this great world.

KNOWING GOD

Daniel 11:32

Introduction
  A. It is important that we understand that knowing about God and knowing God are two totally different things.
    1. We have been looking at some of the things that will help us know God better. We have considered His nature. He is holy. He is kind. He has great plans for us.
      a. We saw that God is holy (Isa. 6).
      b. We felt His kindness (Ezek. 34).
      c. We understand that He is a God who has great plans for us (Jer. 29).
  B. Knowing God personally is the key to our relationship with Him. It is one thing to know about God. Many theologians know about God and spend hours discussing theological attributes. Even some nonreligious people know about God.
    1. Dr. J. I. Packer stated in his book Knowing God: "A little knowledge of God is worth more than a great deal of knowledge about Him."
    2. Daniel gives us great insight into what happens when people know God. Read the scripture: Dan. 11:32.
  C. Consider four true statements about knowing God.

I. A Person Can Know a Great Deal About God Without Much Knowledge of Him
  A. In the Book of Daniel, three kings demonstrate this truth. Nebuchadnezzar knew that God was fully aware of what was going on (Dan. 2). Belshazzar knew that God would not stand idly by and allow items that had been dedicated to Him to be desecrated. Darius knew that God was a lion tamer (chap. 6). Despite all those kings knew about God, none of them knew God.
  B. Daniel and his friends knew God, and that knowledge was the source of their strength, courage, hope, and peace.

II. Those Who Know God Have Great Energy for Serving Him

A. Dan. 11:32 in the RSV reads: "The people who know their God shall stand firm and take action."

B. In the scripture, those who know God cannot rest while He is being defied.

1. Daniel and his friends refused to be part of anything that insulted God.
2. They would not break God's laws and eat forbidden food (1:11-13).
3. Daniel would talk to God (chap. 6).
4. When Darius suspended the practice of prayer, Daniel refused to be intimidated.
5. People who know God are not rebels for the sake of rebellion. They relate to God as naturally as breathing, and the world has trouble with that.

III. Those Who Know God Have Great Thoughts of God

A. In the face of the might and splendor of the Babylonian Empire those who knew God held onto their faith that God ruled.

B. When Daniel interpreted Nebuchadnezzar's dream in 4:26 he said, "Your kingdom will be restored to you when you acknowledge that Heaven rules."

C. God is sovereign.

1. This is the central truth that God taught each king in this book.
2. Note what happens when God is acknowledged (4:34-37).

IV. Those Who Know God Show Great Boldness for Him

A. Daniel and his friends decided that God was in charge.

B. They had a personal knowledge of God, and that was sufficient for them.

Conclusion

A. Those who know God find great contentment in Him.

B. The peace that the Hebrew children experienced in the midst of the most difficult circumstances is still available to us today.

HE KNOWS ME

Psalm 139

Introduction
  A. Last week we looked into the Book of Daniel and the fact that knowing about God is one thing and knowing God is something else.
   1. Daniel and his friends were able to be who they were because they knew God.
   2. The kings of that book knew about God, but those four believers were able to survive fiery furnaces and lions' dens because they knew Him.
   3. Enjoying God begins with the sheer delight of getting to know Him better.
  B. Today, we move to the point that will strengthen our faith. God knows me.
   1. To realize that God knows everything about me and still loves me is marvelous.
   2. As we pursue a relationship with Him, God makes friends with us and draws us to himself so that He can make His love known to us.
   3 In Gal. 4:8-9, Paul does not understand how anyone who has ever known God would not serve Him.

  I. **Throughout His Word God Has Communicated to Humankind, "I Know You"**
  A. Examples:
   1. Exod. 33:11-17—God assured Moses that He knew him.
   2. Jer. 1:5—God assured Jeremiah that He knew him.
   3. John 10:14-15, 27-28—Jesus assured all of us that He knows His sheep.
  B. This knowledge strongly implies personal affection, redeeming action, covenant faithfulness, and providential watch care over those whom He knows.
  C. What really matters is not just that I know God, as wonderful as that is. Even greater is the fact that He knows me.

D. As we look into Ps. 139, we read it in sections and realize that very little comment is needed.

II. He Knows Everything About Me (vv. 1-6)

A. He knows what is going on in my life. There are no secrets from Him (Eccles. 12:14; Matt. 6:4).
B. Our lives are open books before Him.
   1. He knows us so well that even the hairs on our heads are numbered.
   2. He knows our daily activities (vv. 2-3).
   3. According to verse 4, He knows what we are going to say before we utter a word.

III. He Knows Where We Are (vv. 7-12)

A. He knows where we are physically. Illustration: Many airplanes have programs that show where they are at any given moment. God has an even better program. He always knows where we are.
B. He knows where we are emotionally. Illustration: He knew where Elijah was in 1 Kings 19.
C. He knows where we are spiritually.
D. Sometimes Satan clouds our confidence, but God always knows exactly what is going on with us.

IV. He Knows How I Am

A. He knows the talents, gifts, and abilities He has given me. All that He asks is that I become all that He designed me to be.
B. David prays that God will reveal to him things he does not know (vv. 23-24).
   1. In God's sight we are not question marks. We are exclamation points.
   2. If we allow Him, He will tell us everything we need to know about ourselves.

Conclusion

A. God knew us before we were formed in our mothers' wombs. If we will let Him, He will help us understand the plans He has for us.
B. It is encouraging and comforting to know that the God who created the universe has this kind of interest in each one of us.

HE IS A LOVING FATHER

Psalm 103:1-18 (Text Verse 13)

Introduction
A. We will know God better if we understand that He feels toward us like a good father feels toward his children.
  1. Illustration: A pastor observed a young father on a flight from Tel Aviv to Paris. He had taken his nine-month-old son to Israel to show him to his family. The father enjoyed his son's attention and would not even eat until his son was asleep. When the plane landed, he was very careful to put on his son's coat and cap before deplaning. The pastor said to the father, "You seem to enjoy your son." The father replied, "I love him very much. He is the joy of my life."
  2. That is the way God feels toward His children.
B. Children and their parents.
  1. Sometimes children disappoint their parents, but their parents still love them.
  2. Sometimes children bring joy to their parents as they grow spiritually and are happy and mature in their personal lives.
C. Sometimes we treat God as children treat their parents.
D. God wants to help us with a program for life that will bring happiness to us. Three of these areas are pointed out in this psalm. Read the scripture: Ps. 103:1-18.

I. God Forgives Our Sins (v. 3)
A. He forgives every sin.
  1. Note: It is sins, plural. The *Amplified Bible* reads, "Every one of . . ." (AMP).
  2. You cannot name a sin that God has not already forgiven for someone.
  3. Note the good news that David states in verse 10. Thank God that He does not treat us as our sins deserve to be treated.
B. Our sins will haunt us if we let them.

1. While God completely forgives, we may never forget.
2. David said, "I know my transgressions, and my sin is always before me" (Ps. 51:3).
3. The wounds will heal, but scars may very well remain.

II. He Gives Us the Very Best of Life (v. 5)
A. Sometimes we will have difficult situations, such as sorrow and heartache.
   1. How can that be the best of life?
   2. It is the best that life can be under the normal conditions of humanity.
   3. When our hearts ache, our Heavenly Father comes to our aid, and we are renewed.
B. A person's attitude determines the strength and energy that can be received.
   1. If anyone ever had a reason to be distressed at life's situations, it was Joseph. (Study the life of Joseph in Gen. 37—50.)
   2. Through all of his trials, Joseph learned to trust God.
C. A positive attitude toward our Heavenly Father enables us not only to survive but also to soar (Isa. 40:31).

III. God Is Patient with Us (v. 8)
A. He understands our humanity.
   1. He who taught us to forgive 70 times 7 will keep His own standard.
   2. He continues to work with us so that we can achieve His will.
   3. He knows that we are human and not divine.
B. He does not give us what we deserve (v. 10).
   1. How happy we all must be that our Heavenly Father does not punish us in accordance with our failures.
   2. Our Father, like a good earthly father, covets the very best for His children.

Conclusion
A. *The Living Bible*'s translation of verse 13 is beautiful. It reads: "He is like a father to us, tender and sympathetic to those who reverence Him" (TLB).
B. Those who revere God as a Father learn that He is very warm, gentle, loving, and kind.

Understanding God's Permanence

Hebrews 13:8

Introduction
    A. We are heading toward the conclusion of this series on getting to know God.
        1. The more we get to know Him, the more we will trust Him.
        2. We have seen the evidence of these realities through our look at: The names of God, the shepherding heart of God, the God of great plans.
    B. Today we are looking at understanding the fact that God is always the same.
    C. In Bible times, people lived in totally different conditions than those today. They were nomads in tents and lived in a very small world. Because we live in such a different world, we wonder how biblical truths can apply to our lives today. Biblical truths apply to us because human nature has not changed. In spiritual matters, in those areas that determine our relationships with God and toward each other, nothing has changed.
    D. Is the God of the Bible pertinent to our lives today?
        1. The Bible is still a lamp to guide our feet.
        2. Read the scripture: Heb. 13:8. Consider these truths:

I. God Is Everlastingly Present in the World (Ps. 93:1-2)
    A. The Bible attempts to help us understand the eternal existence of God.
        1. Jeremiah calls Him "the eternal King" (Jer. 10:10).
        2. Paul calls Him "the immortal God" (Rom. 1:23).
    B. Created things have a beginning and an ending. The Creator has neither of these. Note the blessing of the realization of the permanence of God in Ps. 102:25-28.

II. God's Character Does Not Change
    A. Some things can change the personality of humans. A kind, loving person can become harsh and critical.

1. This can be caused by several factors, such as a tragedy or illness.
2. But no such thing can happen with God.
  B. The character of God is today and always will be as it is portrayed in the Bible.

III. God's Truth Does Not Change
  A. We live in a world of multiple changes, and the language we use is constantly changing in meaning. Illustration: The word "love" has come to have a variety of meanings today. To genuinely love a person is different from loving an inanimate object.
  B. God's word always means what He intended it to mean (Ps. 119:89-93).

IV. God's Ways Do Not Change
  A. He continues to respond toward sinful people just as He did in biblical accounts.
    1. He hates sin and uses all kind of pain and grief to wean the hearts of His people from disobedience.
    2. Sin is painful and expensive by design (Rom. 6:23).
  B. It is wonderful to know that no repentant person has ever been abused by God. See 1 John 1:9; Rom. 5:9.

V. God's Purposes Do Not Change
  A. Note 1 Sam. 15:29 and Num. 23:19.
  B. What is God's purpose? He created humankind for fellowship.

VI. God's Son Does Not Change
  A. All that Jesus Christ ever was, He still is today (Heb. 13:8). Jesus was and is Savior, Friend, and Good Shepherd.
  B. He still is all of these today and will never change.

Conclusion
Fellowship with God, trusting His Word, living by faith, standing on His promises are essentially the same realities for us today as they were for Old and New Testament believers.

Part II
The Thrill of it All
Discovering and Doing God's Will

Introduction

This series of messages will speak to the pure joy and satisfaction that can be found in fulfilling God's will for our lives. Too many believers struggle in this area of Christian living. Many look at God's will as a "chore" to be carried out. Nothing could be further from the truth.

The will of God may not always be comfortable, but the results of faithfulness in this area are always enriching and rewarding. People who find the pure pleasure of His will for their lives become great attractions to the gospel for others.

These messages address four aspects of discovering and doing God's will. Those who respond will enjoy the thrill of it all.

BECOMING A LIVING SACRIFICE

Romans 12:1-2

Introduction

A. There is no way of living that is more exciting and rewarding than being in the center of God's will.

B. For many people, this is a real battleground.

1. They want to discover and fulfill God's will, but they fail to comprehend how to settle this issue.

2. Sometimes they assume that the will of God always involves full-time ministry of some kind. If that is God's will, He will make it clear.

3. Sometimes the will of God means being a committed layperson who pursues God's will in voluntary service to the Kingdom.

C. In Rom. 12, Paul calls all Christians to the joy of being a living sacrifice.

D. Read the scripture: Rom. 12:1-2.

I. A Myth to Be Exploded

A. Some people assume that the will of God is a life of dullness, denial, and austerity.

1. Nothing could be further from the truth.

2. Carrying out the will of God is the most exciting assignment anyone could have.

B. A look at the call to full-time ministry.

1. Many assume that it is a call to be overworked and underpaid.

2. This simply is not true.

3. Ministry is not a life of richness and prosperity, but God always takes care of those whom He calls.

4. The call of God enables us to contribute the most to His kingdom.

C. The will of God may not involve a call to some area of what we refer to as ministerial work.

1. Every Christian is called to an area of service. There are no spectators in the arena of faith.

2. In answering the call, we share in life's most thrilling experiences.
3. Some people realize little pleasure due to their approach to service.
4. Illustration: Some people have trouble swimming in cool water because they test it for comfort rather than diving in headfirst.

II. How Can We Know God's Will?
A. The will of God is basically a sense of "oughtness."
1. In the case of salvation, we feel the need to be saved.
2. In service to the Lord, we will sense a need to do the work of the Kingdom.
B. Two simple tests can help us prove that it is God's will.
1. God's will is always compatible with His Word.
2. It will always be ethically correct.
It may not always make good sense to onlookers.
C. The voice of God is usually a still, small voice.
1. Elijah's experience in 1 Kings 19.
2. Samuel's call in 1 Sam. 3.
D. We cannot ignorantly miss God's will.
1. Prov. 3:5-6 is a commitment from God.
2. Isa. 30:21 is a commitment from God.
E. Sometimes God has no specific assignment and trusts our judgment and desires.

III. When Will I Know?
A. Frequently, we become impatient with God.
1. We want Him to reveal His plan for us early.
2. He will let us know His plan at just the right time.
3. Illustrate with your call to preach.
B. There is a right time for everything. At the proper time, God will reveal His will.

Conclusion
A. Discovering an area of service for God adds a totally new dimension to our lives.
B. The chorus "To Be Used of God" says it all.
C. When you do this, you become a living sacrifice for Christ.

PURSUING GOD'S WILL

Matthew 7:21-23

Introduction
A. Last week we talked about becoming a living sacrifice to God. We studied about how we can be sure of finding the will of God for our lives. Once we have discovered God's will, we should never look back (Luke 9:62).
B. A call from God is a call to action.
   1. Whatever we do, we must do for the glory of God.
   2. To bring glory to God we must prepare to be the best that we can so that we can serve Him to our greatest potential.
   3. Read the scripture: Matt. 7:21-23.

I. The Preparation Period Can Be a Learning Time
A. Preparation time will teach us that God will provide for our needs.
   1. We can say with Paul, "I can do everything through him who gives me strength" (Phil. 4:13).
   2. We also begin to realize that what God calls us to do, He enables us to do.
   3. As we pursue preparing for His will, He provides needed physical, mental, and emotional strength.
   4. In the spirit of Paul's charge to the Corinthians, whether we are preparing for the ministry or for physical labor, "Whatever you do, do it all for the glory of God" (1 Cor. 10:31).
B. Early experiences help to prepare us for future challenges.
   1. Everything that happens to us is part of God's total picture for us.
   2. Illustration: The pattern of a tapestry is not revealed until the work is completed.
C. After preparation comes the doing.
   1. In our text, Jesus said, "Not everyone who says to me, 'Lord, Lord,' will enter the kingdom of heaven, but only he does the will of my Father who is in heaven" (v. 21).
   2. We are not saved by the work that we do. But our

love for Him compels us to work to demonstrate our love for Him.

II. There Are Many Ways to Be Used by God

A. The first thing to come to mind is always full-time Christian service.
  1. This would mean preaching, missions work, and so forth.
  2. These areas of ministry are critical to the work of the Kingdom.
B. There are a multitude of areas of ministry that depend upon committed laymen.
  1. Read Eph. 4:11-15.
  2. Successful Sunday School classes require dedicated teachers.
  3. We need people who will be active in visitation of shut-ins and those in need.
  4. We must have people who will consistently follow up on newcomers.
  5. We need people who will be part of the ushering and welcome teams.
  6. We must have people who will invest time in musical preparation.

III. Fulfilling Our Ministry May Involve Sacrifices

A. Being a part of ministry involves the sacrificial expenditure of time and energy. When we look at the Cross, it is difficult to say that God is asking too much of us.
B. Doing God's will means that we trust God with the details.
  1. Illustration: The story of the lad at the feeding of the 5,000 reveals that God used the least likely person present to minister to a multitude. The key is: he was used.
  2. We must believe that was the most unforgettable day of that little boy's life.

Conclusion

A. Take another look at Jesus' challenge in the Sermon on the Mount (Matt. 7:21). The vital question is not who we are or our wonderful exploits. The supreme question is: Have we found and done His will?
B. All believers need some way to demonstrate gratitude for their redemption. Pursuing God's will enables us to do this.

DELIGHTING IN HIS WILL

Psalm 37:1-6

Introduction

A. In this message we are looking at the attitude with which we approach God's will.

1. In Ps. 40:8 David wrote, "I desire to do your will, O my God." It is a wonderful thing when we come to the place where we want to do the will of God.

2. Our scripture for today takes our attitude toward God to a higher level.

3. Read the scripture: Ps. 37:1-6.

4. To delight means we find pleasure in doing God's will.

B. Paul challenges our attitude toward the incidents of our lives.

1. Rom. 8:28—Believe it or not!

2. Some people speak the Word better than they live the Word.

3. The beautiful Christian experience that we desire to reach is the spiritual inheritance of each of us through which we discover the pleasure of serving God.

I. Pleasure Can Come from Difficulties

A. Problems are necessary.

1. Trying circumstances help us mature and learn how to handle difficulties.

2. Encountering tough times does not mean that we are out of God's will. Illustration: Job or Elijah.

3. The problems we encounter enable us to realize our dependency on God.

B. Acknowledging our needs causes us to build a strong faith relationship with God.

1. Sometimes people struggle with the temptations of life (1 Cor. 10:13).

2. When the situation seems unbearable, God gives the grace we need for victory.

II. Sometimes the Problems That Arise Are Preparation for Future Blessings

A. In the same way that a potter must exert pressure on the clay to make it what he or she wants it to be, so God sometimes works with us (see Jer. 18:1-6).

B. Financial pressures cause us to depend more on Him for His deliverance. Illustration: Share the story from 1 Kings 17 about how God through Elijah met the material needs of the widow at Zarepheth.

III. The Best Is Yet to Come

A. It is important to have this mind-set if we are going to delight in God's will.

1. "Every Day with Jesus" is more than just a chorus.
2. It is a way of life when we honestly pursue God's will.
3. The miracle of turning water into wine in John 2 demonstrates the fact that the best is yet to come when we do things in accordance with His will.
4. It was the presence of a need that brought about this miracle.

B. His provision is more than adequate.

1. At the feeding of the 5,000 (John 6) there were 12 basketsful left over.
2. The Lord has both quality and quantity.

C. Some people look back for the good days in their lives. In His will we can look to the future with pleasure and expectation.

1. We can have the excitement that Paul expressed in Phil. 3:13-14: "Forgetting what is behind . . . I press on toward the goal to win the prize."
2. This does not mean the end of problems. It means the promise of victory.
3. Difficulties should never disturb us. No opponent—no victory.

Conclusion

A. I really do believe Rom. 8:28. This enables me to delight in doing God's will.

B. The determining factor of what happens in our spiritual lives will be in our attitude toward God.

C. If, like David, our attitude is one of delighting in God, the future will be a thrilling experience.

THE ULTIMATE EXPERIENCE

Esther 4:12-16; 8:15-17

Introduction

A. If you want to live an exciting, rewarding life, find something worth living or dying for and give it all that you have.

  1. One of the great tragedies today is that we can live trivial lives if we wish.

  2. We will live a mediocre life unless we make a deliberate decision to do otherwise.

  3. We must pray that the Lord will help us understand His will for us.

  4. Once we discover that, our attitude becomes one of pleasure in pleasing Him.

  5. That in which I find pleasure I do well.

B. Esther's story illustrates how a young lady found her reason for living.

  1. Read the scripture: Esther 4:12-16 and 8:15-16.

  2. The children of Israel were in captivity in Babylonia.

  3. The penalty of death was upon them. Someone needed to do something.

  4. We cannot estimate what would have happened to the Hebrews without Esther.

C. Let us let the life of Esther tell its beautiful story.

I. The Need for Deliverance (3:8-11)

A. The Jews were in captivity under a godless power.

  1. They had not obeyed God, so He allowed them to be taken captive.

  2. The destruction of the Hebrews was very carefully planned by Haman (3:8-9).

B. This is much like the world in which we live.

  1. There is a godless power determined to destroy all of us.

  2. Satan's infusion of gray into moral areas is the tool he is using today.

II. A Commitment to a Cause (4:16)

A. God spoke to Esther through her Uncle Mordecai.
  1. Esther's first reaction is similar to many of ours—"It's not my problem" (4:11).
  2. Mordecai makes the choice plain (4:14).
  3. Esther realized her personal responsibility and made a total commitment (4:16).
    a. Nothing much happens until we reach this point.
    b. This is the beginning of the blessing of our reason for being.
B. Esther's path is very identifiable.
  1. She and her husband, the king, had a good relationship.
  2. God was with her and became her enabling ability.
  3. Esther used her head in planning to succeed (note Esther 5:4-5, 8; 7:1-3).
  4. The key factor was her total involvement in the cause.
C. Others have been committed. Examples: Moses (Exod. 3) and Isaiah (Isa. 6).
D. The call is very clear to us. We can make a difference.
  1. It is better to die for something than to live for nothing.
  2. If our lives back up our testimony, we have no reason to fear failure.
  3. This is no time for flimsy excuses.

III. Joy Will Come (8:15)

A. Joy came to the Jews.
  1. Esther's commitment resulted in their deliverance.
  2. She had the joy of freeing her loved ones (8:6).
B. Deliverance will come.
  1. God has always had a people, and He always will.
  2. The question is, Will we be a part of His deliverance?

Conclusion

A. It is thrilling to be used of God. The personal satisfaction, peace of mind, and joy of soul is indescribable.
B. We can experience life's ultimate—being used of God.
C. The story of God's people tells the story of people who find a reason for living and pursue it with all of their hearts.

PART III
A FOUNDATION FOR FAITH

Introduction

This series of messages is designed to help establish and strengthen the listeners' faith in some fundamental areas. Like the foundation upon which a building stands, these messages provide support for living. Also, in the same way that a physical foundation determines the size and usefulness of the structure that it supports, this foundation for faith determines the usefulness and size of the spiritual life that is built upon it.

The stronger the foundation is, the stronger the life will be. These messages will enable new and older believers alike to live lives that will lift up Jesus. The truths to which they speak are fundamental to victorious Christian living. When prepared properly in a prayerful mood, these messages will provide a foundation like the one Jesus addressed in Matt. 7:24-27.

Two excellent resources for this series are written by Lee Strobel and published by Zondervan: *The Case for Faith* and *The Case for Christ.*

In the Beginning—God

Genesis 1:1; Psalm 19:1-3

Introduction
   A. A well-lived life, like a well-built building, must have an adequate foundation.
   1. The human structure is one of the most intricate and delicate in the world. This condition demands solid support.
   2. The origin of some mental and emotional problems is the lack of confident support for life.
   3. Rather than raising questions, we need answers.
   4. If intellect is calculated by what a person knows, it is time that we add simple but profound truths to our lives.
   B. Every foundation must have a cornerstone from which the entire structure takes its point of reference.
   1. Today we are going to look at the cornerstone from the Bible.
   2. Read the scripture: Gen. 1:1 and Ps. 19:1-3.

I. A Frank Look at the Reality of God
   A. Let's set the Bible aside for a moment.
   1. We are not setting God aside, but the Bible, because we cannot establish something by beginning with something else that came as a result of its existence.
   2. The Bible is true because God is rather than God exists because the Bible says so.
   B. There are many reasons why some people do not believe.
   1. One is due to the absence of the physical evidence. Yet they acknowledge many forces that are not physical, such as love and hate.
   2. Some struggle over geological age evidence.
   3. Others do not believe because that is a popular response.
   4. The main reason to resist the reality of God is because to admit the reality forces us to face responsibility for the way we live.
   C. Everything must have a beginning.

1. If it was not God in the beginning, what was it? Science has never said.
2. Every theory begins with an assumption. Illustration: Something never comes from nothing. So, what was the point of origin for the universe? For example, what caused the "bang" that many unbelievers cite?
3. We are beginning with God, and that makes everything else possible.
4. Even evolutionists must assume a first cause for the beginning of the process.

II. The Truth About God
A. There are many Christian scientists who believe in God.
B. The scientific description of how the universe began is beyond our comprehension.
  1. Gen. 1:1 is so simple everyone can understand it.
  2. God wrote Gen. 1, and no one could have written it better.
  3. In Ps. 19, David gives us great insights into our universe.
C. The chance of our world coming into existence without divine intervention is beyond our comprehension. We can no more expect our finely tuned universe to have just happened than we can expect the pieces of a great watch to have just come together.
D. Everything becomes simple once our eyes have been opened to our world.
  1. Look at the beauty of nature around us—flowers, trees, birds, and so forth.
  2. The miracle of life itself staggers our minds without a Creator.
  3. The human brain far surpasses any computer. This did not just happen.

Conclusion
A. The existence of a Creator God gives substance to everything else.
B. Once we acknowledge His existence, everything else becomes possible.

The Word of God

Psalm 119:105-112

Introduction

    A. No book in the history of the world has been as thoroughly examined as the Bible. Critics have studied the origin of the Bible in an attempt to expose weaknesses. Believers have studied the origin of the Bible to validate their faith.

    B. No book has endured such a concerted effort to eliminate it. The first manuscripts of the Bible were laboriously handwritten. History records periods when the Bible was banned and burned publicly. For centuries many have given their lives because of their faith in the Bible.

        1. William Tyndale was martyred for translating the Bible.

        2. John Huss was burned at the stake for encouraging people to read the Bible.

    C. This is no ordinary book. The Bible occupies a unique place in history.

    D. Read the scripture: Ps. 119:105-112. Faith in the Bible is a major foundation of our faith.

I. The Nature of God's Word

    A. The purpose of the Bible is to help us understand what God expects of us. The Old Testament gives us the history of God's dealings with the Jews. The New Testament reveals the redemption plan that Jesus provided and the response of those who accepted Him.

    B. The Bible has been given to answer obvious questions.

        1. How did the world begin?

        2. What do we have to look forward to?

    C. The Bible is not an exhaustive history but a selected account of special events. The events of God's activities in history demonstrate how He feels about us. There are unanswered questions, such as, Where did Cain get his wife? There are mysteries such as those found in Daniel and Revelation. In those areas that deal with our salva-

tion, the Book is crystal clear. Rebellion and sin will be punished (Rom. 6:23). Jesus died to solve the sin problem (John 3:16).
  D. The Bible is a very honest book. It reveals both sides of God's nature—love and justice. It contains transparent accounts of the failures of some of its heroes. This is an important factor in validating the authenticity of the Bible.

II. The Authority of the Bible
  A. To understand its authority, we must look at its source.
    1. Paul helps with this in 2 Tim. 3:15-17.
    2. Peter helps with this in 2 Pet. 1:19-21.
    3. The Bible was written by men inspired by God to reveal His truths.
    4. Obviously, Moses was not there in Gen. 1:1. But God inspired him.
    5. The New Testament was written by inspired men according to their personalities.
    6. In the same way that we must understand Jesus as a divine, human Person, so we understand the Bible as a divinely inspired humanly written book.
  B. There are many reasons for believing that the Bible is an accurate account.
    1. Over the centuries no evidence has been found to refute the accuracy of the Bible.
    2. The Jews had strong motives for preserving the accuracy in the Old Testament account.
    3. Under close examination, no error has ever been found in the New Testament.

Conclusion
  A. To believe or not to believe is a decision all of us must make. Admitting the existence of God makes all of the Bible stories possible. Many people have been taught to be skeptics. Therefore, they have no assurances in their lives.
  B. The level of your pleasure in life will be in direct proportion to your confidence in this Book.

The Son of God

Matthew 16:13-17

Introduction

A. The question that is asked in this scripture passage is one that all of us face. Sometimes we prefer to look at what others think about Jesus. In the same way that Jesus personalized this question for Peter, so it is with us. What do I believe? Is Jesus Christ the Son of God? Read the scripture: Matt. 16:13-17.

B. What we are looking at today becomes the third corner in our foundation of faith.

   1. When the truth of His divinity becomes a reality for us, our lives are transformed. Illustration: A brilliant Brahmin scholar in India was disturbed about the progress of Christianity. He planned to distribute a pamphlet exposing the weaknesses of Jesus after spending 11 years researching Him. He failed to find any weaknesses and acknowledged boldly that Jesus was all that He claimed to be.

   2. There are three logical questions concerning Jesus Christ.

I. Was He?

A. Did the Person identified in the Bible as Jesus Christ actually exist?

   1. This is no trivial question. If we acknowledge that He existed, then we are faced with the answer to the question, Is He the Person the Bible says He was?

   2. Admitting the existence of this controversial Person necessitates a decision by us.

   3. The question Jesus asked of Peter is one each of us must respond to.

B. There is no doubt that Jesus Christ lived when and where the Bible indicates.

   1. The facts relating to the historical Christ are as real as any other person in history.

   2. No evidence has ever been presented to even hint that He did not exist.

3. The very nature of Jesus Christ as He relates to Judaism would insure their effort to eliminate the historical Jesus if possible. Yet no such attempt has ever been made.
4. The evidence is overwhelming. Jesus lived when and where the Bible says.

II. Who Was He?

A. This is the question that is raised in our scripture for today. Jesus is asking, What is the attitude of the people toward Me? The response given in verse 14 would have been complimentary to anyone else. Some of today's responses are similar to those. That He was a great teacher and a good man are all great compliments. But these are not enough.

B. Who was He? Look at Peter's response in verse 16.
   1. It is true that He was Mary's Son. The humanity of Jesus is vital. However, Peter's answer, "You are the Christ, the Son of the living God," is the only adequate response. The voice of God on the Mount of Transfiguration (Matt. 17:5) makes it clear that Jesus is more than just a man. Jesus was conceived without the benefit of an earthly father. The Virgin Birth is no problem for our Creator God.

III. Why Was He?

A. He came to reveal God's love for humankind. God is telling us that He has not forgotten us or cast us away. God was reaching through Jesus to humanity to give us a second chance in life.

B. He came to provide redemption for us. We could never do enough to pay for our sins (Eph. 2:8). God built a bridge through Jesus to us so that we might be restored to fellowship with Him.

Conclusion

Jesus Christ is God's love come to earth to solve the sin problem (1 John 4:9). Without Jesus there is no foundation upon which we can build our lives.

The Holy Spirit

John 16:5-16

Introduction

    A. The foundation for faith that we are building is being established on fixed principles that are nonnegotiable. These fixed principles become the pillars of truth on which everything is based. The absence of these principles means that there are no absolutes. Without absolutes, every situation is subject to the mood of the moment.

    B. We have established three corners.

        1. The reality of God.

        2. The validity of the Bible.

        3. The divinity of Jesus.

        4. Today, we acknowledge that the fourth corner is the Person and presence of the Holy Spirit.

        5. Read the scripture: John 16:5-16.

    C. The Holy Spirit is a Person.

        1. He is the third Person of the Trinity.

        2. We cannot cover all facets of the Holy Spirit, but we will reveal the simple truths that will strengthen our spiritual lives.

I. Who Is the Holy Spirit?

    A. He is God.

        1. We do not totally understand because we cannot fully comprehend the Trinity. Yet the clearly established truth of the Bible is that God has chosen to manifest himself three ways—Creator, Son, and Holy Spirit.

        2. When we experience one, we experience all three to some degree.

        3. In the same way that humankind is triune (mind, body, and emotion) yet one, so God is triune (Creator, Son, and Holy Spirit), but He is only one God.

    B. The Spirit was present at the creation (Gen. 1:2).

    C. The Spirit was evidenced in the life of Jesus.

        1. At His conception (Luke 1:35).

2. At His baptism, confirming Him (Matt. 3:16).
3. Driving Him into the wilderness to be tempted (Matt. 4:1).
4. Empowering Him (Luke 4:14-18).
D. It was the work of the Holy Spirit that enabled the Early Church to make an impact on the world (Acts 2ff.).

II. The Work of the Holy Spirit in Our Lives
A. The actions of the Holy Spirit become a vital part of our foundation.
1. Confirming our acceptance as children of God (Rom. 8:14-17).
2. Giving us power to glorify our Heavenly Father (Acts 1:8).
B. Jesus emphasized the importance of the work of the Holy Spirit (John 16:7).
1. The physical Christ was limited to time and space. The Holy Spirit is not.
2. Jesus promised the Holy Spirit in John 14:15-17.
3. Jesus had been with them. The Holy Spirit would be in them.
C. Some important aspects of the Spirit's work.
1. He convicts us of our sins (John 16:8-9).
2. He convinces us of our need for righteousness.
3. He causes those whose eyes are opened to see the advantage of righteousness.
4. He guides us into all truth (John 16:13).
5. He glorifies Jesus through believers (John 16:14-15).
6. He gives us power (Acts 1:8).
7. He gives us peace (John 14:26-27).

Conclusion
A. We can build a great life on the foundation established by these four corners.
1. The fact that God created the world is believable.
2. The Bible explains to us God's plan for His world.
3. Jesus, God's one and only Son, reveals His divine love for us.
4. The Holy Spirit is God in us enabling us to live victoriously in this world.

THE TRUTH ABOUT SIN

Luke 18:18-23

Introduction

A. No foundation for faith is complete without some understanding of humankind's greatest problem—sin.
  1. Unless the guilt and burden of sin can be dealt with, we will be doomed to a miserable life.
  2. A proper understanding of sin will help us build a stable life.
  3. The scripture for today gives a perfect illustration of the results of sinful living.
  4. Read the scripture: Luke 18:18-23.

B. The young man who is the subject of this scripture is proof that nothing can satisfy the deepest longing of the human heart except the assurance of eternal life.
  1. He had everything the world had to offer. Yet he was unhappy.
  2. When he left Jesus, he still had his worldly possessions but was defeated and sorrowful because he refused a change of heart.

C. If your life is ever to become the confident, positive, and pleasure-filled existence it was created to be, the sin problem must be addressed.

D. In this spirit, we will look at sin, its reality, results, and cure.

I. The Reality of Sin

A. Sin is a very real problem in our world and personal lives. The Creator has instilled a basic moral code in every person.

B. Our world has tried to eliminate the stigma that sin produces.
  1. The use of the word "sin" implies moral responsibility.
  2. If they could eliminate this word, they would do away with responsibility.
  3. Truth cannot be eliminated.
  4. We can deny it, ignore it, or change its name. But truth never goes away.

5. Society has tried to turn sin into an illness in order to remove responsibility.
6. Sin is a fact. It is truth, and truth must be faced. It cannot be eliminated.
  C. What is sin?
   1. Webster defines it as, "Disobedience of the divine will."
   2. The very word "sin" carries the connotation of cost, accountability, and penalty.
   3. This strongly implies willful disobedience.
   4. We would like a catalog of specifics, but that is impossible. God gave us consciences that are in tune with His will.
  D. Sin is anything that comes between God and us.
   1. God offered fellowship with himself in return for obedience.
   2. Sin is a reality, and reality cannot be avoided.

II. The Results of Sin
  A. No one has ever been improved by sin.
   1. The young man in this scripture went away unhappy.
   2. Samson disobeyed his commitment to God and ended up in disgrace (Judg. 16).
  B. The consequences of sin. Sin is degrading to the mind and becomes more demanding as time passes. It is destructive to the body. It is damnable to the soul.

III. The Cure for Sin Is Available
  A. Sin is the world's most curable disease.
   1. The cure is stated in 1 John 1:9.
   2. Sin is curable because Jesus went to the Cross to pay the penalty (John 3:16).
  B. We cannot name a sin that has not already been forgiven.
  C. The route to the cure is a simple and honest visit to the Cross.

Conclusion
  A. We can know total release from the guilt, burden, and destruction of sin. Do not deny the reality of sin. Sin is real.
  B. Come to Jesus. He will solve your sin problem, give you peace within and power to live a godly life.
  C. Sin is real and devastating, but because of Jesus it is curable.

The Nature of God

Psalm 103:1-18

Introduction

A. This is the sixth week that we have looked at a foundation for faith.
   1. I hope that you are beginning to see the beauty, simplicity, and personal peace that such a foundation provides.
   2. We are what we are because of what we believe.
B. The cornerstone of life is the reality of God.
   1. It will help us build a better life if we understand His nature.
   2. He is not as the deists would like to claim "a creator who after creation retired to some corner of the universe."
   3. He is a Creator who is still here to watch over His creation.
C. An adequate foundation for life includes more than a Creator God.
   1. It includes an understanding of what God is really like.
   2. David tells us what God is like in Ps. 103. Read the scripture.

I. God Is All-Knowing

A. The very nature of God demands this.
   1. Since God is timeless, yesterday and tomorrow are an eternal "now" with Him.
   2. We can understand this better if we keep in mind that our knowledge is *now*.
   3. This characteristic means that there are no mysteries with Him. He is never surprised at anything that happens in our lives.
B. David says that God knows "me" (Ps. 103:14).
   1. Sometimes we wish people knew and understood us better. He does.
   2. He remembers the frailty of our bodies and the folly of our souls.
C. He knows everything there is to know about us (see Ps. 139).

41

II. He Is All-Powerful

A. Again, the very nature of our Creator God demands this.
1. There are no impossibilities with Him.
2. Since He established the laws of nature, He is in control of them.
3. Illustrations of His power: dividing the Red Sea, crossing the Jordan River, and so forth.

B. Many people are so materialistic that they cannot accept an all-powerful God.
1. As a result of this, they do not believe in miracles.
2. People who never experience miracles in their lives are left at the mercy of material conditions.
3. Believers in a Creator God are not bound to the material laws of the universe because our God is limitless. This means that nothing is impossible.

III. He Is like a Father (v. 13)

A. "Father" was one of Jesus' favorite terms for God.
1. Those who are blessed with good earthly fathers have a great point of reference.
2. Loving fathers understand how God feels toward His children.

B. Look at the attributes of good fathers.
1. Good fathers are forgiving, and so is God (v. 3).
2. Good fathers are patient with their children, and so is God (vv. 8 and 10).
3. Good fathers do not hold grudges against their children, and neither does God (v. 9).
4. Good fathers give the very best they can afford (v. 5 in the *Amplified:* "Who satisfies [your mouth, your necessity and your desire at your personal age] with good; so that your youth, renewed, is like the eagle's [strong, overcoming, soaring]").
5. He loves to be with us. This is why He created Adam and Eve and why He has stayed so close to a world that has rejected Him.

Conclusion

A. People who grasp an understanding of the warmth of God's nature will live in joy, confidence, and peace.

B. The realization that God is too good to do wrong, too wise to make a mistake, and He loves us brings great stability to our lives.

A COMMITMENT WORTH KEEPING

Luke 1:26-38

Introduction

A. This message is the final part of this special series on a foundation for faith.

1. We have looked at: the reality of God who is the cornerstone; the truth of God's Word; the divinity of Jesus; the Holy Spirit; the truth about sin; the nature of God; and a mandate for faith.

2. This last sermon pulls it all together. It is like the final overlapping stone that holds everything else in place.

3. This relates to a question that everyone must answer: What is the focal point of my life? What is my purpose for living?

B. A teenage girl brings us to today's truth. Mary, the mother of Jesus, demonstrates total commitment to God's will. A commitment like Mary's will give everyone a reason to live. Read the scripture: Luke 1:26-38.

I. What Is the Purpose of Your Life?

A. This is a question everyone must answer, for it sets the tone of our lives.

1. Our reason for living is the pattern upon which we lay every decision and action.

2. People without a purpose are like someone building a house without a blueprint. They are like cooks who have no recipe. They are like a song without a melody.

3. We must have something in our lives to serve as a guide.

B. Look at some of the things for which people live.

1. Pleasure—We all know that this is fleeting.

2. Power—This, too, has its limitations.

3. Popularity—One of the most fickle of all patterns.

C. Mary had a reason in her life that would never wear out (v. 38).

1. Her reason for living was to do God's will.

2. What He calls us to do He enables us to do.

3. Opportunities for serving God are never exhausted.
D. The situation for Mary was challenging.
1. Pregnancy without marriage could have resulted in her being stoned to death. She dared to say, "I will take that chance." She trusted God with her life.
2. The "how" of His will was unknown. The "who" was a familiar presence.
E. What is the first question that most people ask when faced with a decision?
1. If it is "What will it cost?" Money is the pattern. This can be taken away.
2. Or, "How long will it take?" Time is the pattern. Time always runs out.
3. Or, "How will it make me feel?" Pleasure is the pattern. This wears off.
4. Or, "What will people think?" Popularity is the pattern. This is fleeting.
5. If by chance we ask, "How will this affect my relationship with God?" then we have established an unchanging pattern that we can use for every decision.
6. Nothing else supports life like this commitment.

II. Blind Commitment Is the Key to Confidence
A. Look at Mary's situation. Most of the women in our world would be glad to exchange places with her. She is honored and revered more than any woman who ever lived. The basis of these honors is found in verse 38: "Whatever you want, God."
B. In the Old Testament, Job's faith was not shaken by the loss of temporal things. Still Job trusted God (see 13:15).
C. God will not ignore the needs of those whose lives are built on total trust in Him.
1. Some would ask about the stoning of Stephen. What a way to go! (Acts 7).
2. How about Paul's problems? Look at 2 Tim. 4:6-8.

Conclusion
A. If we want something stable in our lives, we must sell out to God and trust Him.
B. Mary did, and she became a beautiful illustration of a life that has a commitment worth keeping.

PART IV
MESSAGES THAT ENHANCE CHRISTIAN CHARACTER

Introduction

This section includes three sets of sermon series outlines that will enable Christians to grow in grace. There are three messages in each set. As always, they can be separated and preached as a stand-alone message, but they are stronger when they are kept together. The groups do not necessarily build upon each other, but the messages in each set help form a strong triangle to support our Christian faith.

The three messages on the Love Route, speak to one of the distinguishing characteristics of the people of the Church. Believers who grow in love grow in grace and live in such a way that their faith is attractive to those who are outside of the fellowship of the Church.

The messages of lessons from the Master's miracles teach three very important truths that often escape us. To learn that: Jesus loves life; trouble does not mean that we have sinned and that Jesus loves everyone will lift the lives of those who listen.

The final three messages on maturity will help those who listen to apply the truths and truly "grow in grace." These lessons teach truths that help Christians leave "the milk" of the spiritual nursery for the "meat" that mature believers rightfully enjoy.

As always, personalize these messages with your own illustrations, mix with prayer, and see what God brings forth.

The Love Route—Message One

1 Corinthians 13

Introduction

A. Everyone needs to love and be loved. The quality of our lives is directly affected by the presence of loving relationships.

B. The word "love" is one of the most used and abused in the English language. It is understood by some people as unconquerable benevolence and invincible goodwill. When demonstrated in its finest form, love is a beautiful expression of the way that God feels toward humankind.

C. The best place to learn the true meaning of love is in God's nature.
   1. There are many beautiful illustrations in the Bible: Ruth and Boaz (Book of Ruth); David and Jonathan (1 Sam. 20); God's love for us (John 3:16).
   2. To understand the nature of love that we are to demonstrate toward each other that will transform our Christian lives, we will study 1 Cor. 13 for the next four weeks.

D. The word "love" in English is translated from three different words in the Greek.
   1. *Eros* means lustful desire. It is a self-centered, physical response.
   2. *Phileō* means brotherly love. It is a surface, emotional response.
   3. *Agapē* means unselfish, absorbing love. It comes from the same root as "agony" and is deep-seated passion that has little to do with emotions. Agape love chooses its object and stands by it through thick and thin continually and eternally regardless. This describes God's love for us and the love that we are to have for each other. This is the love spoken of in 1 Cor. 13.

E. Read the scripture: 1 Cor. 13. We begin with verses 1-3.

I. **Love Must Be Sovereign in the Heart (v. 1)**
    A. Silver-tongued orators are just a big noise without love. The power behind our speech is not determined by the extent of our vocabulary but by the depths of our hearts.
    B. Sounding brass and tinkling cymbals are hard sounds that can stir up trouble. Cymbals cannot be tuned. They are designed to be unchangeable. Oratory may command admiration, but only love can reach the heart.
    C. Regardless of how much they are deserved, harsh words do not win the lost. Just because we have silenced people does not mean that we have converted them.

II. **Love Must Be Sovereign in the Intellect (v. 2)**
    A. Mere knowledge will never win anyone to God. Love is the attraction of the gospel. In fact, love is the gospel.
    B. A brilliant mind that can interpret the deepest mysteries of Scripture is useless without a warm, loving heart.
    C. Share some illustrations of people who have knowledge without love.
    D. Apart from love the gifts of the spirit can be used selfishly. A person can become great in religious and other fields of endeavor. But if love is lacking, God is not pleased.

III. **Love Must Be Sovereign in the Will (v. 3)**
    A. Charity without love is useless. Charity can spring from a wrong motive. A person can have an open, lavish hand and still have a cold, selfish heart. Mere sacrifice is not sufficient. Many heathen religions follow sacrifice.
    B. Martyrdom without love is foolishness. Many people who would fight and die for their faith fail to live the essence of Christianity in loving their neighbors.

Conclusion

Notice the four "ifs" of this passage. Notice the four "alls" of this scripture. No one has ever lived who could measure up to all of these without love. But if we could, we would be nothing without love because God is love. Without Him we are nothing.

THE LOVE ROUTE—MESSAGE TWO

1 Corinthians 13

Introduction

   A. Last week we began to look at love. It is a one-word definition of Christianity. It is the stamp of authenticity on all who call themselves Christians. We looked at love by examining verses 1-3. Read the scripture: 1 Cor. 13. Today, we will examine verses 4-7.

   B. Two contrasting pictures are presented in the first half of this chapter. Verses 1-3 present the picture of a talented but unloving person. Verses 4-7 present the picture of a loving person who may or may not be talented.

   C. The loving picture reflects Jesus, and we are to be reprints of Him in our world.

   D. In today's text we are given two aspects of love.
      1. Verses 4-5 reveal the negative side of love.
      2. Verses 6-7 emphasize the positive side of love.

I. The Negative Side of Love (vv. 4-5)

   A. Love does not envy.
      1. "Love is never envious nor boils over with jealousy" (AMP).
      2. Only love can see all of the inequities of life and remain focused.
      3. Where there is no love, there is the seed of envy.
      4. Love is perfectly content in the will of God.

   B. Love is not boastful. Love is not interested in seeking the praise of others. Genuine love develops its own praise.

   C. Love is not proud.
      1. It is not arrogant and inflated with pride. It never looks down on anyone.
      2. Conceited people trample others under their feet. Love tramples no one.
      3. True love raises our attitude toward others and lowers our self-importance.

   D. Love is not rude. It is never ill-mannered. It is always considerate of others.

E. Love is not self-seeking. It does not grasp for its own selfish interests but finds joy in serving others.

F. Love is not easily angered. Simply stated, love does not have a bad temper. Jesus was never vindictive and never retaliated. We are to be like Him.

G. Love keeps no record of wrongs. Since our loving God keeps no records of our forgiven sins, we must follow His example and keep no records of the sins of others.

H. Love does not delight in evil.
   1. It does not enjoy exposing the weakness of others. It weeps over sin and is brokenhearted over failure.
   2. At the Cross, mercy and truth met. Sin was condemned, but sinners were pardoned.

II. The Positive Side of Love (vv. 6-7)

A. Love is patient. It is willing to go the second mile.

B. Love is kind. Enduring wrong could be a triumphant of stubbornness. Kindness is a triumphant of grace.

C. Love always protects. This quality is clearly explained in 1 Pet. 4:8.

D. Love always trusts. Love is not necessarily blind, but it is not suspicious of others. When someone falls, love will think of the battle fought and the struggle he or she went through before the fall. A suspicious person will be a miserable person.

E. Love always hopes. It never gives up on anyone. Love knows that God is able to take the most dysfunctional life and transform it into something beautiful.

F. Love always perseveres. This aspect of love means it cannot be conquered by the weaknesses of others or the circumstances of life.

Conclusion

A. What we have studied today is a photograph of Jesus.

B. We are to be reproductions of Him. Are these qualities found in our lives?

C. Illustrate by describing the love, hope, and patience that a mother demonstrates in treating a child that is seriously ill. This is the way we are to be to others.

The Love Route—Message Three

1 Corinthians 13

Introduction

A. We have been looking at something that is both tough and fragile. Love is tough in that when it is encouraged, many problems that would destroy good people are conquered. It is fragile in that it fails to exist where it is ignored. Love is the stamp of authenticity on Christianity. Our consideration of this great truth will strengthen our personal lives and the church, which is the Body of Christ.

B. We must remember the true nature of this love.
   1. The love demonstrated in this chapter is the same love that God has for us. Therefore, it is not subject to physical circumstances.
   2. Illustration: It may be true that love is blind. When we fall in love we do not focus on imperfections of any kind.

C. The last section of this chapter starts with the declaration, "Love never fails," and ends with the injunction in 14:1, "Follow the way of love."

D. Read the scripture: 1 Cor. 13. Today's text is found in 13:8—14:1.

I. Love Contrasted with the Gifts (v. 8)

A. The people in the Corinthian church were proud of their physical gifts. While this was a talented church, it was a divided church (see 1 Cor. 3). Paul is trying to put everything in a proper perspective and bring everyone together in a Christlike manner.

B. Love and the gifts.
   1. Paul boldly states, "Love never fails." Unfailing love can always be counted on.
   2. Prophecies will cease. A day will come when we will not need prophecy. We will know God personally. We do not need to make prophecy so important since it is temporary.

3. Tongues will cease because heaven will speak one language.
4. Knowledge will vanish. No one can know everything.
5. The marks of imperfection are upon everything except love. Love carries the trademark of eternity.

C. Paul wants the church to grow up (v. 11).
1. We can't remain baby Christians but must mature.
2. Children understand physical things. As we mature we grasp ideas and concepts.
3. Immature Christians can learn to develop childish traits into mature qualities.
4. When Jesus comes and we reach maturity, all gifts will be unnecessary.

D. Heaven will be wonderful (v. 12).
1. It will transcend our fondest dreams.
2. Paul's statement is meaningless unless we really love Jesus. When we do love Him, it thrills our hearts.

II. Love Transcends All of the Other Virtues (v. 13)

A. Love surpasses faith.
1. Faith is essential to our spiritual journey.
2. We do not have to minimize faith and hope in order to exalt love.

B. Love transcends hope. Christian hope is not a vague guess but an absolute, confident assurance. Hope can become a selfish condition without love.

C. The three virtues are intertwined.
1. Faith reaches back to Calvary. Hope reaches forward to heaven. Love dominates our lives in our present world.
2. Faith realizes that Jesus came to save me; hope knows that He is coming again; but love knows that He lives in my heart right now.

Conclusion

A. Love is the greatest of all virtues because God is love. We will never become what He died for us to be until the love of this chapter captivates our souls. We reach this condition by following Paul's admonition in 1 Cor. 14:1a.

B. The world would be a better place in which to live if those of us who are Christians would travel the love route.

Learning from the Master's Miracles—Message One

John 2:1-22

Introduction

A. We are beginning a series of messages focusing on some of the miracles of Jesus.

B. We will be learning truths that will strengthen our faith and enhance our lives.

    1. We believe that God can still do anything He has ever done.

    2. People who do not believe in miracles are robbing themselves of great blessings.

C. There are some truths that apply to every miracle.

    1. In every miracle involving people we see the absolute requirement for obedience. Those who say yes to Him enjoy the benefits of His blessings.

    2. Jesus never did for the people what they could do for themselves. Jesus did not come to make His people helpless but to help them with uncontrollable circumstances.

D. Keep these two lessons in mind as we look at some of the Master's miracles.

E. The Bible records 33 miracles. We are beginning with the first one. Read the scripture: John 2:1-11.

I. Lesson No. 1: Jesus Loved Life

A. Jesus enjoyed being with people and having a good time.

    1. A Jewish wedding is a happy occasion. In Bible days the ceremony lasted a week.

    2. The Pharisees became upset because Jesus partied with Matthew's friends (Matt. 9).

    3. Children are attracted to happy people. They were drawn to Jesus.

B. As followers of Jesus we must exhibit His joy in our lives.

    1. When the world sees that we are enjoying life, they will want what we have.

    2. Christianity is not a condition we achieve because we do not do certain things. Rather, it is a condition we

enjoy because our love for Jesus negates questionable issues.
3. The lifestyle of God's people is one of joy, peace, and happiness.
4. The lifestyle of unbelievers is one of fear and guilt.
5. Jesus loved life. So can we.

II. Lesson No. 2: Life in His Will Gets Better and Better

A. For Christians, the best is yet to come.
1. Our lives should reflect the statement of the master of ceremonies in verse 10 of our text.
2. The sinful lifestyle goes deeper and deeper into heartache and ruin.
B. Across the centuries those who have settled the issue of their faith in God have testified that the longer we live for Jesus, the better our lives become.

III. Lesson No. 3: Accepting What We Do Not Understand

A. The servants enjoyed being a part of this miracle.
1. They obeyed although they did not understand.
2. They knew that it was water that they had put into the water pots.
3. They ran the risk of embarrassment by drawing water to take to the governor.
4. They shared the joy of the occasion.
B. Every miracle demonstrates the need for obedience.
1. At the raising of Lazarus, Jesus had them roll away the stone (John 11).
2. In John 21 Jesus had them put their nets in the water.
3. Jesus told the man by the pool of Bethesda to get up and walk (John 5).

Conclusion

A. When we think of the miracles of Jesus, the greatest one is that He loves us and forgives our sins.
B. The miracle of Jesus' love and grace enables believers to experience life beyond our greatest imagination. Like Jesus, we will have lives filled with joy. Our lives will get better and better as we mature spiritually. Our obedience opens the way for a multitude of options.

Lessons from the Master's Miracles—Message Two

Matthew 14:22-36

Introduction

    A. In this series, we are learning lessons from some of the Master's 33 miracles.

    B. Today we are looking at the miracle of Peter walking on water in Matt. 14.

    C. Read the scripture: Matt. 14:22-36.

    D. We will learn five lessons from this miracle.

I. Lesson No. 1: Trouble Does Not Mean We Have Done Something Wrong

    A. Note the disciples' situation in verse 22.

        1. They had been obedient, and that obedience had put them in jeopardy (v. 24).

        2. Since they had followed His instructions, Jesus took responsibility for their problems. He came to meet them in the midst of their storm.

        3. They were not in jeopardy because of anything wrong that they had done.

    B. We need to learn this important lesson.

        1. According to Matt. 6:45, some difficulties come to all of us.

        2. The assurance of His aid brings great peace in the midst of life's storms.

II. Lesson No. 2: He Knows Where We Are Even When We Don't Know Where He Is

    A. Jesus came to them when they were in need (v. 25).

        1. According to Mark 6:48, Jesus was aware of the intense pressure on His disciples.

        2. He knows what is going on in our lives even before problems arise.

    B. Jesus came to them without their asking for help.

        1. The storm could never be heavy enough to hide them from the eyes of His love.

2. Illustration: Airplanes have a communication system that signals the air traffic controllers who can tell a pilot where the plane is even if the pilot does not know.

III. **Lesson No. 3: Obedient People Walk on Top of Their Troubles**
  A. Jesus enabled Peter to walk on top of the water (vv. 28-29).
    1. Peter's assignment was to simply trust Jesus' instructions and keep his eyes focused on Him.
    2. It was Peter's faith and obedience that enabled him to do the impossible.
  B. How do we survive black nights and cloudy days?
    1. We must simply take God at His word and keep our eyes on Him.
    2. The level of our pleasure in life will be in direct ratio to our confidence in and obedience to His word.

IV. **Lesson No. 4: Weak Faith Creates Problems**
  A. When Peter looked away from Jesus, he began to sink (v. 30). The key to staying on top of our troubles comes from closed-minded faith in God. We must focus on His love, His power, and His presence.
  B. When Peter focused on the storm, his faith failed and he lost the victory.

V. **Lesson No. 5: Jesus Responds Quickly to the Requests of Obedient People**
  A. Peter was exposed to the problem because of his initial obedience.
  B. Jesus responded quickly to his request (vv. 30-31).
  C. There are two key thoughts for us to remember.
    1. They had been exposed to trouble because of their obedience (v. 22).
    2. Obedience to His will is never ignored.

Conclusion
  A. Some people struggle their way through life.
  B. We can walk through the heavy storms of life when we have total trust in Him.
  C. Illustration: Tell the story of the two young women who were held captives in Afghanistan whose faith held steady because they kept their eyes fixed on Jesus.

LESSONS FROM THE MASTER'S MIRACLES—MESSAGE THREE

Mark 5:21-43

Introduction
    A. The overwhelming truth of Jesus' miracles is that He cares for each one of us. There are no unimportant people. You are someone special to Him. The greatest people in history are no more valuable to Him than a small child.

    B. In today's lesson, two miracles are intertwined that illustrate this great truth. Read the scripture: Mark 5:21-43.

I. Lesson No. 1: Everyone Is Important in the Kingdom of God
    A. We would expect Jesus to respond to Jairus. He was a very important man.
        1. He was a ruler in the synagogue.
        2. As a congregational leader he oversaw Scripture reading, prayer, and exhortation.
        3. Jesus did not respond to who he was but to how he was.
        4. Under normal conditions, Jairus would have been in opposition to Jesus. Heartache changes our priorities.
        5. The inference is that Jairus's daughter was critically ill, and he realized that Jesus was his only hope.
        6. Note Jairus's approach to Jesus in verse 22. He humbled himself.
        7. This influential man reached the feeling heart of the Son of God, and Jesus "went with him" (v. 24).
    B. The other person in this passage of scripture did not have the prestige of Jairus.
        1. In that day, women were not considered important.
        2. Occasionally, a woman would rise to the surface of influence (Esther, Ruth, Sarah, etc.).
        3. This woman was so obscure that we do not know her name (vv. 25-27).
        4. According to verse 25, she was ceremonially unclean. Anyone who touched her would become unclean.

5. Jesus does not discriminate against anyone. Gender or conditions make no difference to Him.
6. The woman's problem was as important to her as Jairus's problem was to him.
7. She had faith in Jesus' ability to help her (v. 28).

C. Jesus stopped everything to respond to her need (v. 30).
1. He made it crystal clear that everyone is of equal importance to Him.
2. The Bible is filled with illustrations of Jesus' caring concern: The Syro-Phoenician mother (Mark 7); A variety of needs (Matt. 15).

II. Lesson No. 2: There Are No Impossibilities with Jesus

A. According to this passage in Mark, the woman had a serious problem. In Luke's account there was no medical cure for her illness (Luke 8:43-48). She learned that there are no impossible cases with Jesus. She came in need, she touched in faith, and she left healed.

B. There is no doubt that Jairus had exhausted every available possibility.
1. The best physicians of his day could not help his daughter.
2. He may have heard about Jesus and ignored Him.
3. Desperation makes a difference in our lives.
4. People who place themselves at the feet of Jesus will experience His mercy.
5. Jairus's arrogance was eliminated by his broken heart.
6. The people said, "The girl is dead. Start the funeral" (v. 35).
7. Jesus said, "I have the final word" (v. 36). "Daughter, arise!" (v. 41).
8. She did! (v. 42).

Conclusion

A. There are no impossible cases with Jesus.
1. Sometimes He heals or delivers us from the problems.
2. Other times He performs a greater miracle by giving us the strength to survive. See 2 Cor. 12:7-10.

B. We can experience the same testimony to God's sustaining grace.

LEARNING FROM A MATURE BELIEVER

2 Timothy

Introduction
A. The setting of this passage finds Paul in a Roman jail with no hope of release.
   1. His faith has been subjected to the ultimate test and has been proved to be more than adequate.
   2. In a situation that would normally crush a person, Paul testified with confidence (2 Tim. 4:6-8).
   3. This demonstrates the premier example of spiritual maturity.
B. We, too, can mature in grace to the point where we can live above the situations of our lives.
   1. As Paul wrote in Phil. 4:11, we can "learn to be content."
   2. Maturity enables us to handle anything that life brings our way.
C. We can learn to come into this level of maturity by observing Paul and his advice in this short letter.

I. Look at Paul's Practice
A. He prayed daily (2 Tim. 1:3).
   1. Paul had established a pattern of prayer.
   2. Prayer is the lifeline of God's people.
   3. Illustration: Astronauts working outside of the space capsule have a lifeline connected to the spaceship.
B. Paul is confident regardless of his condition (2 Tim. 1:12).
   1. There are two key phrases of note: "I know" and "I am convinced."
   2. Note the Person with whom we have such a relationship. It is not a creed.
   3. Paul has come to a place where he refused to doubt God's forgiveness.
   4. We, too, can be sure of forgiveness and God's keeping grace.
C. He persevered in the face of persecution (2 Tim. 2:9-10; 3:12).

1. Paul had gotten beyond "fair-weather religion."
2. He recognized that Satan does not back off from believers (2 Tim. 3:12).
3. According to Matt. 5:11-12, we can experience happiness even when we are in the midst of persecution.
   D. Paul knows that he has been faithful (2 Tim. 4:7).
   1. Note the "I haves" of verse 7. This reveals the confidence of his testimony.
   2. There is no greater assurance that we can have.
   3. Knowing that we have been faithful entitles us to experience such a confidence.
   E. Paul is our model for Christian living. Looking at his practice, we see how a Christian must live.

II. Look at Paul's Advice

A. Timothy had been Paul's companion. Paul wanted his son in the faith to enjoy the pleasure of a mature relationship with God. In this final letter, he gives simple advice.
B. "Fan into flame the gift of God" (2 Tim. 1:6).
   1. It takes effort to grow spiritually.
   2. While we are saved by faith, we grow by nurturing that faith.
   3. We must establish daily devotional times with God.
C. Do not be ashamed (2 Tim. 1:8). Hold fast and follow sound teaching (v. 13).
D. Be strong in the spiritual grace that Jesus will provide (2 Tim. 2:1).
E. Be consecrated to the cause (v. 4).
F. Study for improvement (v. 15).
G. Learn what to flee and what to follow (v. 22).

Conclusion

A. Paul became a believer as an adult. Still he established a pattern for his life that boosted him to a level of spiritual strength and maturity.
B. It is not for Paul alone. This opportunity is available to us today if we will listen to his advice and practice those same habits.
C. We may never be jailed for our faith as Paul was, but maturity such as his will enable us to make an impact upon a hostile world.

Practicing Discipline

2 Peter 1:1-11

Introduction

A. We are considering truths that will help us grow in grace and mature in the Spirit.

B. There are several stages in our physical lives, and each one is important. They include childhood, teenage years, and adulthood. There is a natural flow to life, but the important thing is to keep growing.

C. The same principle is true of our spiritual lives. No one goes from being born again to spiritual maturity instantly. We must follow the example of our Master in Luke 2:40.

D. Today, we are taking a logical step that will aid our spiritual maturity—discipline.

E. Peter wrote two letters to believers to encourage them in their Christian journey.
   1. 1 Peter was written to encourage believers in persecution (1 Pet. 1:3-7).
   2. 2 Peter was written to help Christians endure attacks from false teachers.

F. Developing a well-disciplined spiritual life will enhance our Christian maturity. It has been said that the world belongs to the disciplined.

G. There are three important steps found in today's scripture.

H. Read the scripture: 2 Pet. 1:1-11.

I. Step No. 1: Recognizing Divine Resources

A. The divine power (v. 3)
   1. Peter was aware of the power of God. He had seen many miracles.
   2. What do we need in any areas of our lives that He cannot supply?

B. Great and precious promises (v. 4)
   1. This is a priceless resource for those who take advantage of it.

2. Promises that make a difference: for pardon: John 3:16; 1 John 1:9; for provision: John 6:35; for peace: 1 Pet. 5:7; for perseverance: Jude 24.

II. Taking Responsibility for Supplementing Our Faith (vv. 5-7)
A. The responsibility is a personal one.
   1. God never does for us what we can do for ourselves.
   2. Verse 5 clearly states, "Make every effort."
   3. Peter urges believers to add one thing after another to their lives until they are fully equipped with the virtues necessary for Christian living.
B. We are responsible to add goodness (v. 5). Christians are to be good people even when they are under pressure.
C. We are responsible to add knowledge (v. 5). We must work at knowing God and His Word better.
D. We are responsible to add self-control (v. 6). Self-control is vital to maturity in the Christian faith.
E. We are responsible to add patience or perseverance (v. 6).
F. We are responsible to add godliness (v. 6).
G. We are responsible to add brotherly kindness (v. 7). (See 1 John 4:20-21.)
H. We are responsible to add love. We are to live in 1 Cor. 13.

III. The Results of Supplementing Our Faith (vv. 8-11)
A. By recognizing the divine resources and accepting the responsibility for supplementing our faith, the results are wonderful.
B. We gain an effective, productive knowledge of Jesus. We get the entire picture of God's plan for our lives (v. 8).
C. We gain a proper perspective. The NIV reads, "If you do these things, you will never fall" (v. 10). What a wonderful way to live!
D. We make our experience permanent (v. 10).
E. We gain an entrance into heaven (v. 11).

Conclusion
A. While we are saved by faith, we live by exercising our faith in our daily lives.
B. The road of life is cluttered with spiritual casualties. This does not happen when we heed God's Word and practice the discipline that produces a mature Christian life.

Practicing Faithfulness

1 Corinthians 4:1-2

Introduction
A. We have been looking at some areas to help us become mature Christians.
   1. When we studied Paul's imprisonment in Rome, we learned how to maintain our stability in difficult times.
   2. We learned from Peter that discipline is essential in the life of a mature Christian.
   3. Today, we are looking at faithfulness as a step toward Christian maturity.
B. In today's scripture Paul is dealing with a problem that had surfaced in the Corinthian church.
   1. The church at Corinth was immature and divided.
   2. Paul endeavored to address the problems.
C. Read the scripture: 1 Cor. 4:1-2.
D. Faithfulness is one of the hallmarks of Christian maturity.
   1. Faithfulness is critical in any mature relationship.
   2. In order to maintain an orderly society, we must have confidence in each other. Faithfulness encourages confidence.
   3. Life is not easy and requires discipline. This requires us to do certain things because they are right.
   4. Sometimes, faithfulness will make us uncomfortable and inconvenient, but in order for us to discover the greatest potential, we must pursue faithfulness in every area of our lives.
E. We must pity the poor, immature people who have nothing outside of themselves to which they can be faithful. Their lives will be full of selfishness, pettiness, and an underdeveloped character.
F. There are three areas in which each of us is faced with the opportunity to be faithful and thereby display maturity.

I. Faithfulness to Our Families
A. The Bible exalts the family to a position of honor. It is society's basic unit.

1. Destroy this cornerstone and society crumbles.
2. This is why the devil has worked overtime to destroy the family unit.
B. What does it mean to be faithful to our family?
   1. Paul clarifies this in Eph. 5:22—6:4.
   2. Husbands and wives must be faithful to each other.
   3. Parents must be faithful to the trust given to them through their children.

II. Faithfulness to Our Friends

A. A friend is a treasure of immeasurable value. The story of Jonathan and David is one of the most beautiful in all of literature (1 Sam. 20).
B. Our friends bring out the best in us.
   1. Good friends will not only tell us our good points but also point out where we need help.
   2. Good friends pray, encourage, and support each other throughout all of life's phases. Everyone needs friends who help him or her enjoy life.

III. Faithfulness to the Church

A. The level of our spiritual maturity is shown by the degree of faithfulness and commitment to our church. The writer of Heb. 10:25 calls for that.
   1. Can a person be a Christian and not go to church? Yes, but not for long.
   2. Illustration: We can live without food for a while, but not for long.
   3. Why is the church necessary? It is the pattern God chose in the New Testament to propagate the Christian family so that believers can live victorious lives.
   4. We can learn from the biblical patterns of Mary, Joseph, and Jesus (Luke 2:41-42).
   5. Our spiritual success will be directly related to our faithfulness.

Conclusion

A. Faithfulness is not a comfortable topic of discussion but is vital to a healthy and mature spiritual life.
B. Faithfulness is beautiful because it reflects us at our best, and that is what God deserves from us.